MAR - - 2015

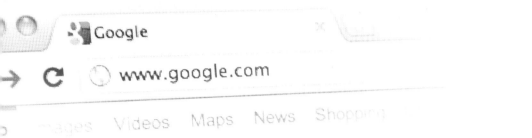

LARRY PAGE

BY SARA GREEN

BELLWETHER MEDIA • MINNEAPOLIS, MN

Jump into the cockpit and take flight with Pilot books. Your journey will take you on high-energy adventures as you learn about all that is wild, weird, fascinating, and fun!

This edition first published in 2015 by Bellwether Media, Inc.

No part of this publication may be reproduced in whole or in part without written permission of the publisher. For information regarding permission, write to Bellwether Media, Inc., Attention: Permissions Department, 5357 Penn Avenue South, Minneapolis, MN 55419.

Library of Congress Cataloging-in-Publication Data

Green, Sara, 1964- author.
  Larry Page / by Sara Green.
    pages cm. – (Pilot. Tech Icons)
  Summary: "Engaging images accompany information about Larry Page. The combination of high-interest subject matter and narrative text is intended for students in grades 3 through 7"– Provided by publisher.
  Audience: Ages 7-12.
  Includes bibliographical references and index.
  ISBN 978-1-60014-990-0 (hardcover : alk. paper)
  1. Page, Larry, 1973–Juvenile literature. 2. Google (Firm)-Juvenile literature. 3. Internet industry-United States–Biography-Juvenile literature. 4. Web search engines-History-Juvenile literature. I. Title.
  QA76.2.P34G74 2014
  338.7'6102504092–dc23
                        2014009919

Printed in the United States of America, North Mankato, MN.

TABLE OF CONTENTS

CHAPTER 1
WHO IS LARRY PAGE?   **4**

CHAPTER 2
A YOUNG LEADER   **8**

CHAPTER 3
**A SEARCH ENGINE
CALLED GOOGLE**   **12**

CHAPTER 4
BRANCHING OUT   **16**

CHAPTER 5
**CARING FOR THE EARTH
AND ITS PEOPLE**   **18**

LIFE TIMELINE   **20**

GLOSSARY   **22**

TO LEARN MORE   **23**

INDEX   **24**

CHAPTER 1

WHO IS LARRY PAGE?

Every day, people use Google to search the Internet. They have Larry Page to thank! In 1996, he and a friend invented the Google **search engine**. It collects and organizes information from the **web**. Today, Google is the world's most popular search engine. Larry is also one of the **co-founders** of the company Google Inc. It is one of the most successful companies on Earth. Google turned Larry into a billionaire at the age of 31. In 2014, he was worth more than $32 billion.

Larry was born on March 26, 1973, in East Lansing, Michigan. His parents, Carl and Gloria Page, taught computer science at Michigan State University. Larry has an older brother named Carl Jr. and a younger sister named Beverly. Larry's parents divorced when he was 8. However, Larry had a happy childhood. He kept a good relationship with both parents.

ICON BIO

Name: Lawrence Edward Page

Nickname: Larry

Birthday: March 26, 1973

Hometown: East Lansing, Michigan

Marital status: Married to Lucy Southworth since December 2007

Children: Two children

Hobbies/ Interests: Kite-boarding, yachting, alternative energy vehicles

"When a really great dream shows up, grab it!"

— Larry Page

From a young age, Larry thrived as a student. His preschool encouraged independent learning and exploring. Larry especially enjoyed taking things apart to see how they were built. When he was growing up, computers were huge and expensive. Most families did not own one. Larry's family was different. When he was 5 years old, his parents bought their first computer. The computer fascinated Larry. He quickly learned how to use it. Soon, he was using the computer to do his elementary school homework.

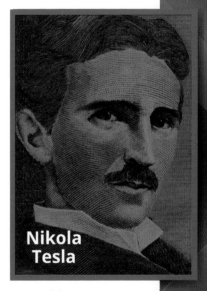

Nikola Tesla

At the age of 12, Larry read a book about Nikola Tesla. Nikola was a brilliant European **physicist**. His discoveries helped create modern electricity. However, he had no business skills and died very poor. Larry was inspired by Nikola's inventions but determined to avoid Nikola's fate. He decided that someday he would turn an invention into a profitable business.

CHAPTER 2

A YOUNG LEADER

In 1991, Larry graduated from East Lansing High School in East Lansing, Michigan. That fall, he moved to Ann Arbor, Michigan, to attend the University of Michigan. He **majored** in engineering. Larry was one of the top students in his class. His classmates elected him president of an **honor society** for computer students. Larry was also in an organization called LeaderShape. Its purpose was to develop future leaders.

On campus, Larry became known for his big ideas. One example involved the transportation system. Larry thought that the campus buses were slow and harmful to the planet. He asked the university to build a **monorail**. It would be a faster and cleaner way for students to get around. Larry did not achieve this goal, but he remained interested in transportation. He joined a school team to design a solar car. It took eleventh place in a worldwide competition for solar cars.

"If you're changing the world, you're working on important things. You're excited to get up in the morning."

— Larry Page

In 1995, Larry graduated from the University with honors. He even received the school's first Outstanding Student Award! Soon after graduating, Larry moved to Palo Alto, California. There, he began a PhD program in computer science at Stanford University.

When Larry arrived at Stanford, a student named Sergey Brin showed him around campus. At first, Larry and Sergey did not get along. However, the two men discovered they shared many interests. Both wanted to work with computers, math, and the web. In time, the two became friends. This friendship would change their lives forever.

LEGO CREATIONS

Larry likes to build things with Legos. When he was in college, he built a printer out of Legos. He also used Legos to build cabinets in the Googleplex campus.

CHAPTER 3

A SEARCH ENGINE CALLED GOOGLE

When Larry began his studies at Stanford, the web was only five years old. Users were still figuring out how to navigate it. Larry chose the web for his PhD research project. His goal was to understand how web sites linked together. This project was complicated and required a lot of math. Larry asked Sergey, a math genius, to help him with it.

With Sergey's help, Larry created PageRank. This system ranked web sites based on the number of their **backlinks**. Larry realized that the web sites with the most backlinks were both popular and useful. He used this information to create a search engine. He called it Google after the mathematical term **googol**. It represented the seemingly endless amount of information on the web. In 1996, the first version of Google went on the Stanford web site. Word quickly spread around campus about Larry's new search engine. Soon, everyone wanted to use it.

GOOGLE IT!

The word *google* is now a verb in the dictionary. It means "to use Google to seek information about a topic on the Internet."

Google was a hit! Larry and Sergey decided to leave Stanford to develop the web site. They raised $1 million from family and friends. With it, they started a company called Google Inc., named after the search engine. In 1998, the men moved to Menlo Park, California. They set up their business in a friend's garage. Larry was Google's **CEO** and Sergey was its president. Users around the world loved the new search engine. It provided top information in a flash. Google quickly expanded. In its first five years, it was one of the fastest-growing companies ever.

A GREAT PLACE TO WORK
The Googleplex has volleyball courts, billiards tables, pianos, and free cafeterias. Google employees, called Googlers, are allowed to bring their dogs to work.

Soon, Larry and Sergey needed more space. In 1999, they moved Google to Mountain View, California. They worked in several buildings that they named the Googleplex. From 2001 to 2011, Larry was the President of Products. Today, he is again the CEO. The company has prospered. In 2013, it earned over $16 billion. Larry's invention is a billion-dollar business!

CHAPTER 4

BRANCHING OUT

Under Larry's leadership, Google developed other services. Today, Google provides email, translation, and map services. People can connect with friends and family on Google's **social media** web sites. One of Google's most popular products is an **operating system** for mobile phones called Android. Google also owns YouTube. This popular web site allows people to upload and watch videos.

Larry has already achieved great success. However, he continues to seek ways to improve people's lives. To do this, he challenges himself and his employees to come up with new ideas. Some day, people may be riding in Google's self-driving cars. People are currently testing them on roads in several states. A Google company called Calico aims to help people live longer, healthier lives. Google is also interested in **artificial intelligence**. In the future, Google may offer devices that can quickly learn information about their users. This will help them provide better services.

A BUCK A YEAR
Larry's annual salary is just $1 a year. He also refuses bonuses. His income depends on how well the company does in the stock market.

CHAPTER 5

CARING FOR THE EARTH AND ITS PEOPLE

Larry cares about the future of Earth. He is a fan of alternative energy. His house in California has solar panels and a rooftop garden. Solar panels also line the rooftops of many buildings on the Google campus. In 2006, Larry **invested** millions of dollars in Tesla Motors. This company makes electric cars. Google is also part owner of the world's largest solar power plant in California's Mojave Desert. It helps provide energy for 140,000 homes.

DO YOU HEAR BLEATS?

Goats graze the grounds of the Googleplex. They act as lawn mowers to keep the grass short.

Larry gives back in other ways as well. In 2005, he and Sergey created a charitable **foundation** called Google.org. It promotes the use of technology to solve global problems. The foundation has given hundreds of millions of dollars to different organizations around the world. Some of these protect children and wildlife. Others help communities hit by disasters. The foundation also helps improve Internet access in poor countries. Larry's commitment to Google.org is helping to change the world for the better.

RESUME

Education

1995-1998: Stanford University, M.S. Computer Science (Palo Alto, California)

1991-1995: University of Michigan, B.S. Engineering (Ann Arbor, Michigan)

1987-1991: East Lansing High School (East Lansing, Michigan)

Work Experience

2011-present: CEO of Google

2001-2011: President of Products, Google

1998-2001: CEO of Google

Community Service/Philanthropy

2014: Donated more than $177 million to various charities

2012: Donated nearly $124 million to the Carl Victor Page Memorial Foundation

2005: Established Google.org foundation; committed nearly $1 billion to charities around the world

LIFE TIMELINE

March 26, 1973:
Born in East Lansing, Michigan

1991:
Graduates from East Lansing High School, East Lansing, Michigan

1995:
Graduates from the University of Michigan, Ann Arbor, Michigan

Spring 1995:
Meets Sergey Brin at Stanford University

August 1996:
First version of Google is available to Stanford University students

www.google.com

Maps   News   Shopping   Gmail   more ▾

May 2009:
Receives an honorary doctorate from the University of Michigan

September 7, 1998:
Launches Google Inc. with Sergey

April 4, 2011:
Becomes CEO of Google Inc.

December 8, 2007:
Marries Lucy Southworth

November 2009:
Forbes magazine ranks Larry and Sergey fifth on a list of the most powerful people in the world

March 2014:
Ranked number 17 on *Forbes'* list of the world's billionaires with a net worth of $32.3 billion

GLOSSARY

artificial intelligence—an area of computer science that deals with giving machines the ability to seem like they have human intelligence

backlinks—incoming links from web pages to other web sites; backlinks determine how popular a web site will be.

CEO—Chief Executive Officer; the CEO is the highest-ranking person in a company.

co-founders—people who start a company with other people

foundation—an organization that provides funds to other charitable organizations

googol—the mathematical term for a one followed by 100 zeros, or 10^{100}

honor society—an organization for high school or college students who earn good grades

invested—put money into a business or idea

majored—studied for a specific degree

monorail—a railroad where the track consists of a single rail, typically high off the ground

operating system—the main program in a computer that controls the way it works; an operating system makes it possible for other computer programs to function.

physicist—a scientist who studies matter, energy, motion, and force

search engine—a program that collects and organizes information from the Internet

social media—web sites and other technologies that allow users to connect with one another

web—an information system on the Internet that allows documents to be linked to other documents; web is short for World Wide Web.

w.google.co

os Maps News

TO LEARN MORE

AT THE LIBRARY

Flammang, James M. *Larry Page and Sergey Brin*. Ann Arbor, Mich.: Cherry Lake Pub., 2008.

Green, Sara. *Sergey Brin*. Minneapolis, Minn.: Bellwether Media, 2015.

Sutherland, Adam. *The Story of Google*. New York, N.Y.: Rosen Central, 2012.

ON THE WEB

Learning more about Larry Page is as easy as 1, 2, 3.

1. Go to www.factsurfer.com.

2. Enter "Larry Page" into the search box.

3. Click the "Surf" button and you will see a list of related web sites.

With factsurfer.com, finding more information is just a click away.

INDEX

alternative energy, 18

Android, 16

awards, 11

Brin, Sergey, 11, 12, 15, 19

Calico, 16

childhood, 4, 7

East Lansing High School, 8

education, 7, 8, 11, 12

family, 4, 7

Google, 4, 12, 13, 15, 16, 18

Google.org, 19

Googleplex, 11, 15, 18

hobbies, 7, 8, 11

Internet, 4, 13, 19

LeaderShape, 8

Michigan State University, 4

PageRank, 12

philanthropy, 19

self-driving cars, 16

services, 16

Stanford University, 11, 12, 15

Tesla Motors, 18

Tesla, Nikola, 7

timeline, 20-21

University of Michigan, 8, 11

web, 4, 11, 12

worth, 4, 15, 17

YouTube, 16

w.google.com

os   Maps   News